ANTHONY RIZZO IS A GOOD ITALIAN BOY

Amanda ReCupido & Matt Lynch

illustrated by
Jillian Solarczyk

Anthony Rizzo is a great
baseball player.

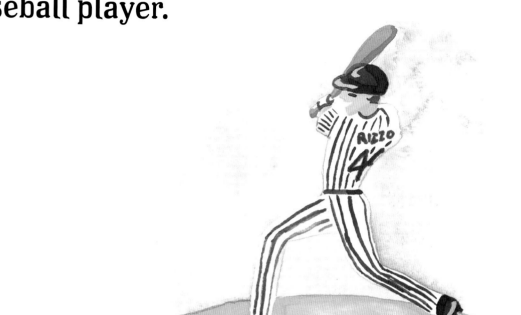

Anthony Rizzo plays
first base for the
Chicago Cubs.

But Anthony Rizzo is also something else...

A good Italian boy.

Good Italian boys spend time with their family.

Anthony Rizzo helps set the table for big Sunday dinners with his family. He always finishes his plate—especially the sauce!

Good Italian boys get along with their brothers and sisters.

When Anthony Rizzo and his brother both want the last cannoli, Anthony suggests splitting it.

He even lets his brother have the bigger piece!

Good Italian boys know when it's time to be silly.

Anthony Rizzo likes to sing and dance with his friends.

It doesn't matter if you're the best, just as long as you're having fun!

Good Italian boys also know when it's time to work hard.

Anthony Rizzo practices baseball every day, so he's always getting better at fielding and hitting home runs.

He likes hitting home runs the best!

Good Italian boys have a positive attitude.

When Anthony Rizzo was younger and became very sick, he always looked on the bright side, and it helped him get better.

Good Italian boys help others stay positive, too.

Because Anthony Rizzo knows what it's like to be sick, he tries to help other people get better. He reads books like *Strega Nona* to kids when they're in the hospital, and they always end up smiling!

Good Italian boys follow the rules.

When **A**nthony **R**izzo's playing baseball, he listens to the umpire.

When he's at home, he listens to his mother. No tiramisu before dinner!

Good Italian boys aren't afraid to try new things.

Anthony Rizzo will even try anchovies on his pizza. You never know what you'll like unless you try it!

Good Italian boys help their friends.

When one of his teammates has a bad game, Anthony Rizzo is always there to tell him that he'll do better next time.

Sometimes he tells a funny joke to make them laugh and feel better!

And good Italian boys always put family first.

Anthony Rizzo doesn't always get his way, but he tries not to complain. He's grateful for all the good things in life—his friends, his amazing job with the Chicago Cubs, his health, and of course...

... his big

Italian family!

Photo credit: Hannah Drews Photography

About the Authors

Matt Lynch and Amanda ReCupido are a husband and wife team of writers, humorists, and die-hard Cubs fans living in the Chicago area. They love spending time with family, especially when pasta is involved!

Photo credit: Leigh Kunkel

About the Illustrator

Jillian Solarczyk is an illustrator and art director from the Chicago area. She grew up in a family of loyal Cubs fans, despite living in the south suburbs. She also knows when it's time to be silly, just like Anthony Rizzo!